This book is not for the reading. Please discard.
If you do not discard, then please draw on the pages.
Decorate this book in doodle.

Then give this book to someone you like.

You and I wrote it together.

Each one is unique. As unique as you make it. As
unique as you are.

LLAMA DISCO PICNIC

Scott Autrey

llama disco picnic

Be more than an excuse.

If you were strong enough and brave enough to get on the horse, then you are strong enough and brave enough to pick yourself back up after getting bucked. Don't forget your strength and courage just because you're on the opposite end of where you want to be. Because it's ONLY that strength and courage that's going to get you back on top. Fight for it. Furrow your brow, set your jaw, grit your teeth and get up. Let's go. We don't have time for this. There's work to be done.

People tell me that they want to see more. This is very easy to accomplish. The harder you look, the longer you look, the more you will see. There's a whole universe in a single blade of grass, and all of the wisdom of the world in a single petal. Keep looking and you'll keepings seeing.

We take so very much for granted. We pass beauty and pay it no attention. We are always so busy, headed somewhere to do something. We don't even look around us. We seldom stop. But we should stop every now and again and just look. There's a gorgeous world around us. Miracles abound. How can anyone feel anything but blown away by the stunning elegance of this beautiful globe? We are truly blessed. Don't take this blessing for granted. Look at it. Experience it. Be a part of the beauty of its world as much as it is a part of yours.

I know the best people. Thank you all for being who you are. Each and every one of you.

Oh I would say that many people are not yet who they are to be. Clay and not yet golem. I know so many wonderful people who just need that one break, that one word, that one moment that takes a person from what they are, into what they are supposed to be. The metamorphosis cocoon to butterfly. I've watched so many people blossom, come into their own. I've watched comedians on tiny little stages become international entertainers, I've watched people who thought they could - do. I've seen tears in people eyes fighting to make things happen, and tears in their eyes when they did. I know the best people, and I have seen them do incredible things. It is a glorious thing to watch. To encourage another. To succeed and in success pave the way for another. And I have seen people bursting with potential - so frustrated at that potential that they give up. But you can't give up. Not on yourself, not on your dreams. You just can't wait for your dreams to come true - you have to make them come true. And the beauty of that is that the only person who can stop you is you. Step aside and let the real you step forward, into the future you deserve. Claim it. Conquer it. Earn it. I know the best people. I'm glad you are one of them.

In reality, no one that matters will fault you for that which you can't do. But will wait patiently for that which you haven't done. It's wasn't about what you can't do. You're lying. It's about what you refuse to acknowledge that you can do. It's about what you haven't pushed yourself to do yet. You wanna be the best? Stop saying you can't. I DON'T CARE ABOUT CAN'T. I care about can. Just because you haven't doesn't mean you can't. Just because you don't think you can doesn't mean you can't. You are more than you know. Start believing in you like everyone around you that matters believes in you. And those that don't believe in you, get them quickly out of your life.

The strongest people in the world are those that make those around them strong, so that in moments of weakness, they are surrounded by strength, inspiration, and heart.

Some people live their lives like an open book. Nothing wrong with that. But it's your responsibility to whoever you want reading to make that book interesting. Of what use an open book, if no one wants to read it.

Anyone that knows me knows that they don't know me, it's the only way to know me. Ya know?

Sometimes you have to drop your pride and blindly forgive, if what's being offered is worth that. Know your worth. And know the value to you of that which you want.

I was wrong. I thought you could rule the world. You can't even return a phone call. I was way off.

Sometimes you can stretch your arms out. Sometimes this will lift you off the ground and you can soar. ... When you do this, remember to look down and acknowledge the people who are holding you up while you soar.

She wrote the word "peace" all over her body and walked out onto the battlefield. But peace was not found on the battlefield and the message did little good for the world when only seen by those who followed orders.

There are many things that I am thankful for. I don't need a day for that. I need a lifetime.

Your video should be as powerful as your audio. Make your words worth something. Make your actions worthwhile.

Accept it or change it. No whining.

Other people can't define you. You can't live your life to someone else's mold. You have to be you. And you have to be okay with that. People come and go. But you gotta live with you forever. Be happy with the self you got.

Be awesome at everything you can, be excellent to one another, and love and respect yourself - and you'll never once have to beg for attention.

This is not your miracle year. It's not lucky or special. Things will not be different. The only thing different about today is what you choose to make different.

There will be hardships. You can let them be your master, or you can choose to be the master of them. Success will be available if you choose to take it. You can choose to give. You can choose to accept. You can choose to win. You can choose anything.

Chances are, most of you will choose to do everything the same. If you had an amazing 2011, then that's awesome. But if it wasn't, it's time now to choose awesome. Or, you can choose to struggle in vain.

What will you decide? Oh what will you decide? Not making a decision is a decision not to be any better than what you currently are.

Be confident that you're worth an amazing year but humble enough to realize that no one owes you one.

But strong enough to let nothing stand in your way,
but gentle enough to lend a hand.

Be comfortable enough to be yourself, but not so proud as to not want self-improvement.

Be financially secure, but make time for life along the way.

Be good to those that are good to you, and remove yourself from those that only wish to tear you down.

Watch what you eat, but eat what you find delicious.

The things you have forgiven, forget. The things that you held in hatred in your heart, let go. You don't need it anymore.

If you want to be heard, start by listening. If you want what you say to matter, say less.

Clean away the clutter in your room, house, car, office, mind, soul, life. If you have no use for it, then it has no purpose.

Don't be afraid to try things you don't think you'll like. Be afraid to have missed an opportunity or an experience because you had the wrong notion about it.

Travel. See something. Make a memory. Learn a craft. Learn a language.

Be on time to things scheduled. Take your time with things that arent.

Be patient but dont wait forever.

If its not worth your time, don't waste your time. And don't make believe that something is worth your time that you aren't enjoying.

Be okay turning things down for better things, but don't turn down everything until there's nothing left.

Be okay accepting things.

Don't choose friends that you want to change. You can't, they can't, the end. Accept them and if you can't and you don't like them, then end it. It's futile. Give up. Move on.

Show your gratitude. Show your thanks. Show appreciation. Saying thank you is the least you can do, but is that how low your appreciation is?

This will be just as amazing a year as you are as a person. Make the right choice.

I don't know how things are going to work out today, but I know they are gonna. It may not be exactly the way I wanted it to, but they will work out.

Where there is a serious why, there will be an accommodating how.

I will will it into existence. I will believe it into being.

I am undaunted. I am unafraid. I will succeed. I will be victorious.

Someone asked me "what is the sound of one hand clapping?" to which I replied "whoosh" and I inquired of them "what is the sound of one clap handing... Over their wallet to me? Don't make any sudden moves, this is a hold up" to which they replied "you're weird" and left. Also none of that happened but MAN it would have made for a mildly rousing campfire tale.

I don't get offended when you stare at my nimbus cloud. I'm just saiyan.

I want it.

Regardless of the consequence, do what you feel is the right thing to do. (not think, feel) Often both options seem right, often neither seems right. There is a price for doing the right thing. There is also a reward.

When you don't have the answers, there is no shame in asking questions.

Stand by your conviction. Forgive yourself for doing whatever you must do.

Be strong.

I am thankful to my maker, for all the making. Not bad, maker. Not bad at all.

You ARE what your silliness defines you as.

Well, today has been filled with all sorts of disappointment. Down, but not out. Still smiling. I will squeeze awesomeness out of this tube of despair. Oh there's joy somewhere, and I'm gonna find it.

Apparently I can only summarize my frustrations by using toothpaste dispensary metaphors.

Maybe If you seem to be finding it difficult to spring back up -after you've fallen -then maybe your falling on the wrong things.

Maybe your falling for the wrong things.

I've known times where i've seen a pile of rocks, and knew I'd get hurt diving in, but dove in anyway, hoping for the best.

That which makes you weird makes you awesome.

The people who embrace their crazy can control it, are a master of it. The people who try to reject it are a slave to it and are controlled by it.

When you're a gypsy, the thought of running away is kinda like thinking hey it's Thursday.

I was feeling good. Then i heard news that made me feel even better. Then i kinda got down. and hearing this latest news, I felt even worse. i felt abandoned, but I felt like I was correct in feeling that way. I felt like I had been passed by, but i stood by my conviction. So then i decided to just be a be a star.

or in other news....

My day has been kinda

Up, Up, Down, Down, Left, Right, Left, Right, B A Star (t)

I dont want to procrastinate. I'm terrible at it. I want to do something fun. or if not fun exciting, or if not exciting something involving sushi, a russian ballerina, a can of instant coffee, a car whose battery has died and looping christmas carols on bad speakers.

The sun comes up, but I don't hear birds chirping in the morning anymore. What now heralds the day? The lights were up, but the sound is not working.

Anything you build, someone will want to destroy. anything you destroy, someone will want to build. But since everyone is just inside your own head, you should figure out what exactly you do want.

I think you should probably give someone a chance first. Before you start trying to change someone, you should probably get to know them first. Take chances. Be patient. You may discover something great that you never knew you wanted. It's hypocritical to celebrate your own weirdness without being open to others individuality. When you can let people be their own people, then you can learn to appreciate them for who they are.

We are all a part, but we are all apart. you can never truly know fully another person. There are always surprises. It's the most beautiful part of it all.

Today is going to be awful. I hate opposite day. It sucks.

The only way to climb a ladder is to start climbing. Planning and doubting alone never got anyone to their goal. It's time to climb. And the only way to do it, is to do it.

The sky is covered in clouds tonight. No star winks through. And moonlight settles on the tops of the clouds that absorb it like a sopping wet wad of paper towels. It's the rain season here. I don't see the moon, and that moon don't see me. Mostly, on account of moons ain't got eyes.

Do you remember it, or do you just remember the story of it?

You can change the world. And really, you're the only one can change your world. Isn't it time?

www.ingramcontent.com/pod-product-compliance
Lightning Source LLC
Chambersburg PA
CBHW061516180526
45171CB00001B/203